The Sower and the Seeds

Matthew 13:1-23

RETOLD BY MARY BERENDES • ILLUSTRATED BY ROBERT SQUIER

Distributed by The Child's World®
1980 Lookout Drive • Mankato, MN 56003-1705
800-599-READ • www.childsworld.com

ACKNOWLEDGMENTS
The Child's World®: Mary Berendes, Publishing Director
The Design Lab: Art Direction and Design
Red Line Editorial: Contributing Editor
Natalie Mortensen: Contributing Editor

LIBRARY OF CONGRESS CATALOGING-IN-PUBLICATION DATA
Berendes, Mary.
  The sower and the seeds / by Mary Berendes; illustrated by Robert Squier.
     p. cm.
  ISBN 978-1-60954-394-5 (library reinforced: alk. paper)
  1. Sower (Parable)—Juvenile literature. I. Squier, Robert. II. Title.
  BT378.S7B47 2011
  226.8'09505—dc22   2011004959

Printed in the United States of America in Mankato, Minnesota.
July 2011
PA02087

The parables of the Bible are simple, easy-to-remember stories that Jesus told. Even though the stories are simple, they have deeper meanings.

One day while Jesus was sitting by the sea, a great crowd gathered around him. He told them this story:

———◆———

There was once a sower who went out into his field to plant his crops. As the sower sprinkled the seeds, he did not pay attention. The seeds were going everywhere!

Some of the seeds fell onto the road. Hungry birds flew down and ate all these seeds right away.

Some of the seeds landed
on rocky ground. These seeds
grew quickly over the next few
days. But soon the hot sun
burned their leaves and roots.
The young plants died.

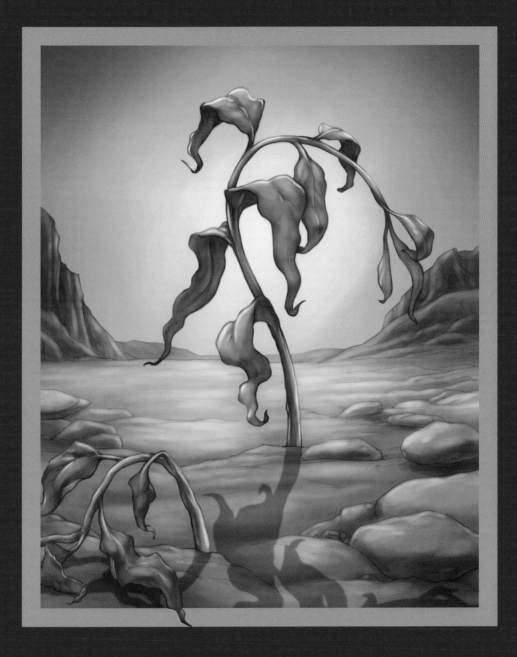

Some of the seeds landed among thorns. These young plants grew taller, but soon the thick thorns choked them. These plants did not grow any fruit.

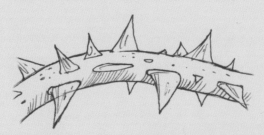

But some of the seeds landed in good soil. These plants grew healthy and green. Some produced 100 fruits, some produced 60, and some produced 30.

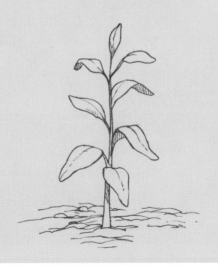

"Jesus," asked his friend,
"why did you tell us this story?"
"To help others understand
God," said Jesus.

"When people do not hear or understand God's message, they are like the seeds on the road—evil snatches them up right away. When people hear God, but pay attention only for a little while, they are like the seeds in the rocks.

When people hear God
and lead good lives at first—
but then begin to care more
for money and lies, they are
like the seeds in the thorns.
But when people hear God's
message and are good and
kind all their lives, they are
like the seeds in the good soil."

BEYOND THE STORY

Jesus often used fruit-bearing trees to help explain what his stories meant because the image was one everyone understood. Many of the people Jesus preached to were farmers. They grew food for their families to eat or to sell at the market.

Every farmer knows how important good soil is. Plants need the nutrients they find in the ground to grow. They get this food and water through their roots. If a farmer is careless about where he places his seeds, the plants will not grow. Many will be sickly and produce no fruit. Some will wither and die. It is only the plants that the farmer cares for lovingly by placing them in good soil that grow. When they receive all the necessary ingredients, they grow strong and produce fruit.

Jesus compares his followers and the way they hear his message to the different ways a seed can grow. Some people refuse to hear the word of God. They cannot learn God's message; they are like the seeds that are eaten by the birds. Some people don't pay close attention to God's message. They start out enthusiastically, but they are easily distracted and their minds wander. These people have shallow roots to their faith. Their faith often withers and dies like the seeds among the rocks. Other followers are so busy with other things, they don't have time to listen to God's word. Like the plants growing among the thorns, all of the distractions in their lives keep them from bearing fruit. Jesus tells us that in order to grow and thrive and bear fruit like the seed in good soil, we need to have an open mind. We need to be willing to listen in order to understand. We need to never be too proud or too busy to learn. Then we will grow strong roots and our faith will bear fruit. When we hear God's will and live according to it, we will reach our full potential.

Mary Berendes has authored dozens of books for children, including nature titles as well as books about countries and holidays. She loves to collect antique books and has some that are almost 200 years old. Mary lives in Minnesota.

Robert Squier has been drawing ever since he could hold a crayon. Today, instead of using crayons, he uses pencils, paint, and the computer. Robert lives in New Hampshire with his wife.